Crunch and Munch

Written by Nora Sands

Contents

Collins

No-cook Cooking!

Here are four **recipes** for you to make.

They're so easy – you don't even have to cook them!

You will need:

a measuring jug

a big mixing bowl

a teaspoon

a grater

a lemon squeezer

a tablespoon

a jam jar with a lid

Remember!

* Make sure an adult does the chopping. Don't use a sharp knife by yourself.
* Always wash your hands before touching food.
* Don't use nuts in your recipe if anyone is **allergic** to them.

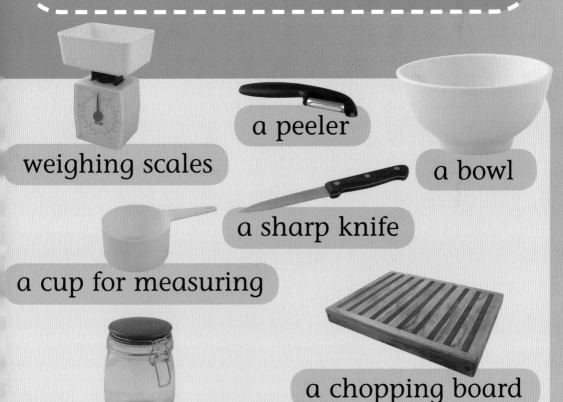

weighing scales

a peeler

a bowl

a sharp knife

a cup for measuring

a chopping board

an **airtight container**

Morning Munch

Here's a crunchy, munchy breakfast to start off your day.

You will need:

* 150g porridge oats
* 150g dried fruit, nuts and seeds
* some milk
* a teaspoonful of honey
* fresh fruit (washed and chopped)

This makes enough for four people.

What to do:

1. Weigh the oats, dried fruit, nuts and seeds.

2. Put them all in a big mixing bowl.

3. Mix with a spoon, or with your hands.

4. Put some of the mixture in a smaller bowl.

5. Pour milk over it.

6. Add some fresh fruit and honey on top.

7. Crunch and munch!

Top Tip

If there's any dry Morning Munch left over, put it in an airtight container. It'll stay fresh for a week.

Carrot Crunch

This recipe is bright, juicy and easy to make.

You will need:

* 1 lemon, cut in half
* 1 orange, cut in half
* 100ml olive oil
* 3 large carrots (peeled and grated)
* 100g currants
* fresh mint leaves (torn)
* salt and pepper

This makes enough for four people.

What to do:

1. Weigh the currants.
2. Measure the olive oil in the measuring jug.
3. Squeeze the orange and lemon in the lemon squeezer.
4. Pour the juice into a mixing bowl.
5. Tear the mint leaves.
6. Add the olive oil, grated carrots, currants and torn mint.
7. Sprinkle with a bit of salt and pepper.
8. Mix everything together with a spoon.
9. Enjoy!

Top Tip

Eat this straight away
when it's fresh.

Super Salad Dressing

You can make a salad even tastier with this lemon and honey salad dressing.

You will need:

* juice of 1 lemon
* 4 tablespoons of honey
* 1 teaspoon of mustard
* a pinch of salt and pepper
* 1 cup of olive oil
* a clean jam jar with a lid

This makes enough for four people.

What to do:

1. Put everything into the jam jar.
2. Screw the lid on the jar very tightly.
3. Shake, shake, shake!
4. Put some dressing on your salad.
5. Crunch and munch!

Top Tip

Put the jar with any leftover dressing in the fridge. It'll stay fresh for a day or two.

Rainbow Kebabs

Here are some fruit kebabs
to make your tastebuds tingle.

What you need:

* wooden **skewers**
* any type of washed fruit, such as:
  * apples
  * bananas
  * oranges
  * grapes
  * raspberries
  * kiwis
  * strawberries
  * grapefruit

* For a sauce:
  * yoghurt
  * honey

What to do:

1. Choose your fruit.
2. Peel or remove the skin if you need to.
3. Cut the large fruit into bite-sized chunks.
4. If you have chosen oranges or grapefruit, separate the **segments**.
5. Small fruit like strawberries, raspberries and grapes don't need to be cut.
6. Push the fruit chunks carefully onto the wooden skewers, in any order you like.

7.   Then mix up some yoghurt and honey in a little bowl ... dip, and eat!

19

Glossary

airtight container
a plastic box with a lid that won't let the air in

allergic If you are allergic to something you become ill when you eat or touch it.

recipes lists of foods and instructions for making things to eat

segments small pieces of an orange or grapefruit

skewers thin sticks with pointed ends

Index

A poster

Come to the Crunchy Munchy café in the school hall.

═ Menu ═

Breakfast **Morning Munch**
a crunchy, munchy breakfast
to start your day

Lunch **Carrot Crunch**
a bright, juicy salad

Super Salad Dressing
with lemon and honey to
make a salad even tastier

Dessert **Rainbow Kebabs**
a fruit dessert with a yummy
dipping sauce

Come and munch!

Café open
8.30am – 9.30am
12pm – 1.30pm

 Ideas for reading

Written by Linda Pagett B.Ed (hons), M.Ed
Lecturer and Educational Consultant

Reading objectives:
- be encouraged to link what they read or hear read to their own experiences
- discuss the significance of the title and events
- listen to and discuss a wide range of non-fiction
- apply phonic knowledge and skills as the route to decode words

Spoken language objectives:
- participate in discussions, presentations and debates
- give well-structured descriptions, explanations and narratives for different purposes
- maintain attention and participate actively in collaborative conversations

Curriculum links: Science; Humans and other animals

High frequency words: they, little, with, day, can, two, your, then, when, that, on, come, and, put, over, in, what, four, it, some, this, them, your, the, do, to, off, if, don't, with, or, a, by, I, would, have, in, my, been, to, here, are, four, for, this, you, to, make, so, them, will, big, with, an, all, put

Interest words: allergic, kebab, airtight container, kiwis, yoghurt, segments, skewers

Resources: small whiteboards, ingredients for recipes (optional)

Word count: 539

Build a context for reading

- Discuss making meals with the children. Ask: *Who has prepared any? What have you prepared? Have you used a recipe?*

- Explain that you are going to read through some recipes and discuss how they are written.

- Discuss the title. Does this give a clue about the sort of food in the recipes? Are there any clues in the cover picture?

- Ask the children what features would be helpful to the reader in a recipe.

- Give one recipe to each pair of children to read through and decide if the food is interesting, if it is something they might like to eat and if the recipe has helpful features.

Understand and apply reading strategies

- Hear the children read in turn. Prompt and praise use of phonic strategies to decode unknown words.